# SALCOMBE HARBOUR REMEMBERED

## Muriel and David Murch and Len Fairweather

Salcombe Harbour from Sharpitor (mid 1920s).

This version of the book is virtually as originally published, presenting the work of
Muriel and David Murch and Len Fairweather.
There are now additional pages at the back providing information about the publisher, Arthur L Clamp.

The republishing project is being managed by Arthur's grandson, Steven Gibson. We aim to find all the research
that he was involved in publishing, preserving it for the next generation as part of 'The Clamp Collection'.

## INTRODUCTION

FOR Maritime Heritage Year we decided to produce a record of the maritime history of Salcombe using old photographs many of which have been on display in the Salcombe Maritime and Local History Museum for the last six years. Once again we have relied heavily on those taken by A. E. Fairweather and Len Fairweather. Those before the turn of the century were taken by T. Partridge and some from "Kingsbridge Estuary" written by S. P. Fox and published in 1864.

There have been many changes to the Salcombe waterfront since World War Two, the most noticeable being the construction of the Creek car and boat park and the road to Batson. It has become apparent that there were many changes during the nineteenth and early part of this century. Bigger yards were required when trade flourished and larger vessels were needed. To acquire more space the shipyards were extended by reclaiming the foreshore. Between 1796 and 1887 at least 200 vessels of differing sizes and rigs were launched from Salcombe yards. From 1837 to 1912 at least 86 were launched from the Kingsbridge yard.

There was employment for some 200 men in these local yards. Men were also employed as sailmakers in four lofts in Salcombe and at two in Kingsbridge. There were those who specialised in making spars, masts, blocks, pumps, casks and even trennels (tree nails—wooden nails). In 1851 there were three shipsmiths in Salcombe and the iron foundry at Kingsbridge provided ironwork. Kingsbridge had two rope-walks, the first was established in 1783, the second shortly after the end of the Napoleonic Wars. So far we have not found any written record of rope-walks in Salcombe.

In April, 1866, and again in May, 1872, the shipwrights of the Salcombe yards came out on strike. In 1866 they asked for 20 shillings instead of 18 shillings for a 72 hour week. They went back to work without getting a rise in pay. In 1872 they asked for 1d per hour increase and to leave work on Saturdays at 4 p.m. Eventually they settled for ½d, per hour rise and a 70 hour week.

In 1848, 355 vessels entered the harbour with 16,723 tons of cargo consisting of coal, timber, groceries and fruit. 211 vessels took away 7,269 tons of corn, flour, malt, potatoes, slate and cider. The remainder sailed in ballast. The increasing prosperity of the port continued until 1864 when 98 foreign-going vessels were operating from the port and nearly as many coastal and harbour vessels. Well over 1,000 seamen were involved at any given time.

Although the number of vessels being built in Salcombe was about three vessels every two years from each yard, the output could barely keep pace with the losses occurring. The vessels were commanded and crewed by local seamen, often three generations of one family serving on one vessel. The loss of a vessel with all hands often meant that the male line of a family ceased. The greatest loss of vessels occurred during one gale on 15th November, 1851, when seven local vessels were wrecked off Terceira, Azores. Despite such calamities there was never a shortage of crews. One can imagine the anxieties of the womenfolk as they scanned the shipping news in the local papers for reports of ships that were long overdue. There were many vessels lost with all hands or reported sailing from a port and not heard of again. Those fortunate to survive the rigours of this way of life often did well. The majority of the Victorian houses seen in Salcombe today were built by shipowners and masters.

The decline of wooden sailing ships which was occurring all around the coast due to the advent of steam and steel framed and hulled vessels was obvious at Salcombe from 1879. The result was less work in the yards both in new construction and repairs. Vessels were laid up in the harbour or sold to foreign ports. The seamen and craftsmen emigrated to the deep sea fishing ports or to dockyards.

© 1982: Muriel and David Murch,
Len Fairweather.

### ACKNOWLEDGEMENTS

Crown copyright is acknowledged for the extract of the crew list of the barquentine *Brizo* dated January, 1879, and held by the Devon Record Office. They appear by permission of the Controller of H.M. Stationery Office.

Extracts from the Salcombe Harbour Notice 1011/A/D/SS, dated 10th June, 1844, deposited by the late W. G. Jerwood, M.B.E., of Kingsbridge, are reproduced by permission of the Devon Record Office.

The two ferry boat pictures taken by the late Edward Chapman are reproduced with the kind permission of his grandson Robert Chapman, photographer, at Plymouth.

We received help from numerous local families who have supplied details and dates, and the use of Fairweather photographs the glass negatives of which were lost when Salcombe was bombed in World War Two.

A Salcombe pilot was taking this brigantine out over the Bar at the entrance to Salcombe Harbour. His boat is being towed behind the vessel. The coastline in the background shows the cliffs from Jones' wall to Prawle Island.

The outward bound ketch had just passed between Old Harry and Blackstone Rocks. The beacons were first erected on the rocks in 1844. The bay is South Sands where stands the old Lifeboat House.

The vessel was the locally registered fishing schooner S.E. 29. The building on the point was a magazine for the Coastguard battery which mounted one gun in 1849 and two by 1860. The man sculling was E. Quick of Salcombe who often fished off Lambury Point.

The three masted topsail, schooner *Romanic* of Antwerp was being towed to sea in 1926. She had discharged her cargo of bricks at Salcombe. They were required to build West View Terrace.

Smacks and ketches wait for a breeze to spring up. One crewman attempts to tow a ketch to sea. These vessels usually had a master and one crew, c. 1890.

Fresh south-westerlies fill the sails of vessels beating out of the harbour, c. 1900.

In 1861 a battery of two 32 pound muzzle-loading cannon, manned by the 10th. Devon Artillery Volunteers (Salcombe), was established at Castle Point. It superseded the Coastguard defences on Lambury Point. The field of fire extended out over the Bar some 1500 yards. This area is still known as the Range.

Children watch the annual inspection of the Volunteers on 28th September, 1883. The men hold handspikes, rammers and sponges. At a later date the pillbox hats were replaced by police-type helmets. On parade were three officers, five sergeants and twenty-six gunners. Eight were absent with leave, two absent without leave.

The flagpole shows the position of the battery. The cannon were withdrawn from service during the early 1900s. Here today stands Castle Point Hotel which overlooks Fort Charles built in 1544 and known as the "Old Bulworke" when rebuilt in 1643. It provided a safe haven for Royalist frigates. The Royalist garrison withstood a four-month siege in 1645. They were bombarded by Parliamentary forces encamped on the cliffs above Lambury Point.

During the 1800s and early 1900s the leading marks for vessels entering the harbour were a white mark painted on North Sands sea wall which was lined up with Landmark Beacon. The beacon was prominently positioned on the skyline above North Sands Valley. The stone base of the beacon is still at Landmark Corner. The picture below shows the view from near the beacon at the turn of the century before houses were built and trees planted. Note the farm gate near Sandhills Corner to keep cattle from straying into gardens. Two rows of tree trunks on North Sands beach helped to dissipate the strength of the waves before they reached the sea wall.

LOWER PART OF SALCOMBE HARBOUR No. 11

In the late nineteenth century as many as 200 sailing ships used the harbour, from the Bag to Mill Bay, as a safe haven during stormy weather. Within half a century pleasure craft had replaced the trading vessels.

The little castle standing on Limpyer Rocks was one of the defences built at the beginning of the Napoleonic Wars. Its purpose was to convince the French that the harbour was well fortified. It was manned by militia in 1802 and known then as "the battery". From here a salute was fired on receipt of the news that Mafeking had been relieved on 17th May, 1900.

The 1824 etching shows the natural cliff below "Old Cliff House" and the path from Baker's Well leading to the ferry landing. The rowing ferry crossed the harbour to Ivy Cove. Some mock fortifications can be seen. One of the buildings at South Orestone is the Commercial Inn, 1739.

The sea wall was constructed pre-1842 and the land was terraced to become the lower garden of Cliff House. At the northern end of the wall the Coastguard Armoury was built on the site of an old lime kiln, c. 1830. At the same time, on the other side of the public steps, a small Coastguard Station House was erected. Later it was replaced by a Coastguard Watch House. The steps became the new ferry landing.

This close-up view of the South Orestone area shows the armoury with its flagpole, the public steps and the Coastguard Station House. Then come the Ferry Cottages, dated 1739, and the *Commercial Inn*, now the *Ferry Inn*, whose earliest known licensee was Mrs Ann Ingram, 1842.

The late eighteenth century Grange still overlooks this area. The pier had not been built when this photograph was taken.

A cobbled lane in front of the inn and Ferry Cottages led to the Coastguard Watch House and the Armoury.

The pier was built in 1871 by George Steer and Sons of Salcombe. The cost was met by public subscription, the Steamship Company contributing the greater portion. But for objections lodged by trading vessel owners, the pier would have been some twenty feet longer. The stones used in its construction were quarried at Lambury.

The original steps, made of Cornish granite, were on the town side of the pier. In 1887 a second flight was constructed on the seaward side. Later the same year, to commemorate Queen Victoria's Jubilee, ornamental harbour lights were erected. Early this century the memorial lights were replaced by a new set designed and made by T. A. Teague a local blacksmith.

The earliest recorded ferryman was Edward Ball. He was followed by "Chummy" Weymouth and Ben Clarke seen here wearing his leather seaboots.

Below is Ferryman Distin who manned the last rowing ferry. The fare was 1d. return. The transome of the boat is displayed by the Salcombe Museum Society in their summer exhibition.

In 1911 Commander S. W. Ryder of York Hotel, now Salcombe Hotel, bought the ferry rights and introduced a 20 foot two cylinder motor ferry boat named *King George V*. The return journey by motor ferry took 5 minutes and the fare remained at 1d. return. It was operated by Jim Cannam until he was drowned when the Salcombe lifeboat, *William and Emma* capsized near the Bar 27th October, 1916.

10

This etching is reputed to be of Salcombe showing the rugged cliffs of Bolt Head and a few houses around South Orestone.

Below: The waterfront c. 1876, from the pier to Fishpond Corner, showing the shipyards on which the prosperity of the town depended.

The small boats moored in the harbour emphasise the fact that by 1920 the remaining shipyards were building small craft and fishing boats.

In 1911, out of a fleet of 60 boats, only three crabbers were not motorised. Motor power brought about rapid development to the design of the boats. The fishermen found it was possible to work twice the number of pots with less labour.

Here the paddle steamer *Kenwith Castle* heads for Kingsbridge whilst the *Ilton Castle* lies at her moorings.

To the right of the pier was a sail loft. The close-up shows Nicholas Trute, the proprietor, and his staff of four journeymen and two apprentices. Next door was the workshop of William Patey, a pump and blockmaker.

Lying off the pier is the last vessel built by James Vivian, the 231 ton barquentine *Brizo*. She was built for Balkwill and Company of Kingsbridge and was launched in March, 1877. In 1879 her crew was: Caleb Gillard, mate; Roger Pepperell, bosun; John Murch, cook/steward; William Hannaford, A.B.; F. Peterson, Aaron Murch and John Pepperell, O.S. She sailed to Bermuda, the West Indies and Brazil.

By the late eighteenth century there were two, possibly three, established shipyards. In 1796 the 35 ton sloop *Kingsbridge* was launched. Early in the nineteenth century two yards were operating on the site now occupied by the Salcombe Hotel.

John Ball and family had the southernmost yard. A John Ball, shipbuilder, died in 1808. It is known from port registers that another John Ball built 19 vessels between 1826 and 1838, the largest being the 172 ton schooner *Era*.

Edward Pepperell had the yard about 1840 and J. H. Patey in 1860. The yard proved too small when there was a demand for longer vessels and Patey used his skills to repair and reclass vessels. The yard became defunct in the 1870s.

The other site was occupied by Thomas Hatch who was reputed to have built fine foreign-going vessels. As he worked before the earliest surviving port registers little is known about his activities. When he failed in business William Bonker and James Vivian took over the premises. As partners they launched three vessels between 1826 and 1829. During this partnership Vivian opened a new yard on an adjacent property in 1828. Bonker continued in business and built at least twenty-four vessels before being declared bankrupt in 1868. His last and largest vessel, the 242 ton *Annie*, was registered as a "three masted brigantine". The bowsprit of his schooner *Zouave* extended across Fore Street and into the window of a house.

The yard was taken over by Henry Harnden and George Whiddon who had been building on separate sites at The Island. The partnership lasted until 1870 when they were declared bankrupt and the yard probably closed down. Harnden continued at the family site at Island Quay until 1887.

At his new yard James Vivian built forty-four vessels between 1828 and 1877. All but one were locally owned. The largest vessel ever launched by local shipbuilders came from his yard. It was the 550 ton barque *Ocean Belle*, 161 feet in length. He died during the construction of his last vessel the *Brizo*. The yard was bought for £665 on 5th. January, 1877, by William Date of Kingsbridge because his yard there was too busy to accommodate the construction of another vessel. Here Date built the brigantine *Sarah Jane*.

In the early 1880s the yard was acquired by William Chant. By this time shipbuilding in the harbour was on the decline. He turned to boatbuilding and repairs to small craft. William's son, Philip Edwin, was able to persuade only one son, his third, Joseph, to work with him. Joseph continued the family business until his death in 1954. Then the yard was incorporated with the Salcombe Hotel and was made into a carpark and boat store.

At Council Quay, now Whitestrand, John Evans senior had a thriving business by 1815 when he launched the 74 ton schooner *Amelia*. The business prospered for three generations. At least thirty-four vessels were built. John Evans junior enlarged the yard in 1848 by reclaiming the foreshore. Thomas Murch hauled 176 cartloads of rubble to fill out the site. Joseph Evans launched his last vessel, the 289 ton brig *Creole*, in April, 1878. She was built for R. H. Sladen of Salcombe.

T. Saunders took over the yard and launched the 70 ton sloop *Lucy* the following February. His second and last vessel was the schooner *Lord Devon*.

In 1889 Aaron Dornom senior moved from Feofee Quay to part of the site. He repaired and reclassed vessels and built Admiralty whalers and cutters. The business was passed on to his three sons Aaron junior, Sidney and Wilfred and subsequently his grandsons worked there until 1968. The yard was used by various firms and finally by Peter Taylor as a boatyard for some years. Luxury flats were built on the site in 1981.

Harry Cook took over the other part of Evans' yard for pleasure boat hire.

Cook's Boathouse and Dornom's boatyard on the site of Evans' shipyard.

Aaron Dornom, senior, who started the boatbuilding business, is standing with his apprentices. From left to right are Weymouth Johnson, Aaron's son, Wilfred, Edgar Cove, Fred Heath and Frederic Muren, c. 1901.

A shark caught in the harbour was displayed on Harry Cook's quay, 1906. Viewing the catch are, on the left, Alban Pepperell, a shipsmith, Aaron Dornom, junior, and Sidney Lapthorne the boatman wearing a peak cap. The two children sitting on a canoe are Ashley and Florence Cook.

Council Quay is now Normandy Way. The old gentleman carrying a basket was Pilot Robert Foale. On the right is the extended Dornom's Yard partially covered to provide storage for boats during the winter.

The horse hauled a cartload of stones for the construction of a new retaining wall to enlarge the shipyard and to build Council Quay. c. 1890.

The building on the foreshore in the centre of the picture was shipsmith Samuel Wills' forge where five men were employed in 1851. Alban Pepperell took over the smithy during the 1880s and continued the business until 1906. The property was then incorporated with Dornoms' yard.

The 114 ton topsail schooner *Lord Devon*, launched in April, 1885, is seen berthed on the foreshore off Foily Quay. She was the only vessel specifically built for the Salcombe Shipowning Company and the last trading vessel built at Salcombe for local owners. When photographed her master was Captain W. H. Leaman and her crew were E. Hannaford, R. Bull, W. W. Yelland and W. T. Way.

Elliott reclaimed a portion of the foreshore and made a quay, c. 1800. Here Thomas Cousins had a pump and blockmaker's workshop.

Elliott erected a room on this site which served a double purpose, as a school during the week and on Sundays as a Methodist preaching place. Houses built there were known as Elliott's Court. Later he built more and now all are known as Clifton Place. The slipway is known as Chapel End because a Chapel of Ease, built in 1401, overlooked this area.

On Custom House, Steamer or Trinick's Quay are sacks of merchandise piled against Balkwill's store. The first floor was used by carpenter and undertaker J. P. Cranch and his son, Alfred. In 1910 the top floor area was used by the Liberal Club. A topsail schooner is alongside *King's Arms* or Packet Quay.

The new Custom House was built 1847/8 in Valentine Place now Union Street. Reeves timber store, now Cooks' boat store, was a sail loft built for Thomas Partridge, sailmaker, in 1827.

Below: The 247 ton brig *Okenbury* is being reclassed at Victoria Quay. In the background is Harnden's shipyard where she was built in 1869.

The small picture above and the one to the right show vessels under construction at Harnden's Island Quay yard, now Edgar Cove's boatyard. Edgar Cove started boatbuilding at the head of Shadycombe Creek in 1909 and in June, 1920, he extended his business to Island Quay.

From Island Quay yard Harnden launched his last vessel in September, 1887. She was the 141 ton schooner *Pearl* built for out-of-port owners. She was the last trading vessel to be built at Salcombe.

The site was used by "Wrecker" Distin as a storage depot for salvaged materials during the early part of this century. His salvage vessel *Elcho Castle* is alongside the quay in Breakwater or Quick's Bay.

This view taken after World War One shows Custom House Quay, Victoria Quay and Victoria Place which was destroyed by enemy action in the last war. Then come Edgar Cove's new boathouse, Island House, and the wall of the fishpond built by John Harnden during the latter part of the nineteenth century.

The fishpond was built on foreshore rented from the Duchy of Cornwall at 5/- per annum. John Harnden's experiment for storing live fish proved unsuccessful. Two of his fleet of fishing vessels are lying against the quay.

The fishpond wall on the extreme left was breached to provide a small haven. The long grey-roofed building was William Thorning's sail loft. Further along was Brewery Quay. The lines of washing indicate the site of the local laundry.

The London sailing barge *Runic*, possibly laden with coal, waits for the tide to rise in Snadycombe Creek to enable her to berth alongside a quay. Smoke rises from the fire at the local refuse tip. Here began the reclamation of the foreshore which today provides a car and boat park and a road to Batson, c. early 1920s.

This was Snadycombe Creek before the tree-lined foreshore was developed and Island Street extended to join Gould Road, c. 1895. The gasworks, lower right, were built in 1866.

The partly dismantled hulk of the *Lady Kinsale* was lying on the foreshore at the head of Shadycombe Creek. She was a sloop of 58 tons built by Bonker in 1843. She was broken up completely in 1871.

These three World War One destroyers beached in Batson Creek, two near the lifeboat stocks and one below Croft Fields, were broken up by "Wrecker" Distin.

A clam, an ancient manmade pathway over the mud, crosses the creek to a point near Snapes Farm. It was used frequently by seamen as a short cut to Salcombe when their vessels were at anchor in the Bag.

Wiscombe lime kiln is a typical example of 25 or more kilns around the estuary. They were situated on the foreshore to facilitate the unloading of the barges which brought the limestone from Plymouth. The centre of the kiln comprised of a large hopper into which layers of sticks, coal and the limestone were loaded from above. The kiln was fired for a day or more and the resulting burnt lime was raked from the hole deep inside the archway. The lime was used mostly for agricultural purposes and for building.

The 310 ton barque *Malborough*, 118 feet in length, built by Vivian, was launched by Mrs. R. Foale on 16th September, 1870. Her husband was a shareholder of the vessel. The barque was built for E. Jarvis and Company of Kingsbridge and her master was William Weymouth. She was sold to Grimsby in 1882 and was transferred to Norwegian registry in 1890.

Among the vessels lying in the harbour are the ketches *Shortest Day* and *Eclipse* and the barges *Yealm*, *Phoenix*, *Emma* and *J.N.R.*

The *Kingsbridge Packet* entering the Bag will pass a few boats moored between Snapes Point and Black Knob Point. Beyond are Tosnos and Gerston Point with Kingsbridge in the distance. Returning, on the other side, are Charleton, Wareham and Halwell Points. Next is Quarantine Bay where ships were segregated until granted pratique. Then come Ox Point and Scoble Point.

Kingsbridge and Dodbrooke are situated at the head of the estuary. The logs and sawn timber, salting and seasoning in the mud belonged to Date's shipyard which was a little further down the creek towards Salcombe. A smack can be seen berthed at Dodbrooke Quay.

The local ketch *Effort* and the topsail schooner *Moss Rose* are alongside Bond's or New Quay. The *Kingsbridge Packet* is near the Packet Store and in the distance there is a vessel under repair.

The 85 ton ketch *Effort*, 67 feet in length, was built by William Date in 1880. Those having shares in the vessel were William Date, Henry Grant, corn merchant, John Lidstone, sailmaker, Thomas Rich, ropemaker, and William John Thomas, shipowner—all of Kingsbridge. Others with shares were William S. Hannaford, butcher, and Edison Lapthorne, master mariner and captain, both of Salcombe. The stevedores had a welcome break from work to pose for the photographer. The gentleman wearing a boater was William Bond and Captain Lapthorne has a peak cap with a bobble.

A small steam tug tows a three-masted schooner away from the quayside. A brigantine and a ketch are still secured. The flat-bottomed barge moored by the steps was used during channel clearing operations in the estuary.

Below: This shipyard was the site of John Jordain's timber yard when he was engaged in housebuilding. During 1837 it was suggested that there was more profit to be made building ships. Consequently a shipyard evolved and Jordain was accredited with eleven vessels launched from the yard.

In 1846 Henry Martin, shipbuilder of Dodbrooke, launched the schooner *Salcombe Castle* from this same yard. She was lost on the coast of New Zealand on 15th September, 1863.

However in 1847 William Date was recorded in the Dartmouth Port Register as having launched his first vessel, the 120 ton schooner, *Compeer*. She was lost with all hands after leaving the Azores in 1858. The Date family are known to have built 74 vessels. The shipyard closed down a few years before World War One.

The ribs of a vessel under construction are probably those of the *Little Gem*, c. 1893.

The *Appona* was built by Date and launched in 1869. She was a 180 foot brig of 188 tons and cost £4,000. She sustained damage when in collision with a Dutch vessel near Lundy. This photograph was taken the same year. A local newspaper reported on 14th June, 1871, that she sailed from Haiti for Salcombe with a cargo on 2nd April, 1871 and it was feared that she was lost with all hands. The mate and most of the crew came from Salcombe. She was never heard of again.

The swing bridge across Bowcombe Creek, originally known as Charleton Bridge, was constructed by A. Saunders, millwright and engineer, in 1845. It was pivoted on a race of twelve cannon balls. The swing section was necessary to maintain the right of navigation to the head of the creek. This waterway was used for the transportation of slate from Buckland-Tout-Saints quarries as well as agricultural produce.

The Salstone Rock near the entrance to Frogmore Creek, being extra-parochial, became the place of worship for Non-conformists during the years of religious persecution from 1662 until the Declaration of Indulgence issued in 1687. Until the mid-1930s Nonconformists maintained a wooden cross on their rock as a memorial to their martyred ancestors.

Molescombe Quarry was opened in Henry VIII's reign and worked spasmodically. The quarry was in operation during 1864. It was one of several quarries which exported slate by barge from Frogmore Creek.

The expanse of water in this area is known as Widegates.

A tidal salt marsh in South Pool Creek was reclaimed by building an embankment in 1806. This was breached in the 1930s and quantities of earth removed to make a yacht basin for S. I. MacDonald of Gullet.

South Pool, situated at the head of the creek, owes its name to Lord Nicholas de la Pola, lord of the manor during the reign of Henry I. His son went with Richard I to the Holy Land. The village supplied one vessel of 50 tons and men to fight against the Armada in 1588.

The large elm tree was much prized by the villagers, but apart from providing a meeting place, it does not appear to have had any special significance.

The local paddle steamers which plied between Kingsbridge and Salcombe would make excursions to South Pool village during the summer when tides permitted. The *Ilton Castle* is passing Gullet Farm.

A number of farmhouses at Gullet have been devastated by fire. They were typical Devon cob and thatch houses built near the water's edge and surrounded by orchards and woodland. The construction of the present house commenced in 1925. A road and agricultural cottages were also built for workers on Gullet Estate.

The other arm of South Pool Creek leads to Goodshelter and Waterhead. At Goodshelter there is a farmhouse and a few cottages built on the side of the hill overlooking the little bay. At the end of the creek is Waterhead where there are a few cottages and an old mill with its waterwheel abutting on to the foreshore.

Around the turn of the century William Lamble Yabsley, a noted agricultural engineer, utilized water power to drive engineering plant and a saw mill of his own design and construction. The water was obtained from a spring which rose in the high ground behind the mill. He supplied sawn timber and coffin boards to Salcombe. With his steam tractor and portable saw he felled and transported trees from local woods to his saw mill. He also had a small casting foundry.

The pathway from the front gate of this picturesque cottage at Waterhead leads to a clam which crosses the creek and connects with the footpath to South Pool.

26

Jim Stone had a boathouse at Long Park between Dutch End and Horsepool in 1935. After World War Two he took over what had been Giles' Coal Store at Goodshelter for a boatyard. The family are renowned for their Salcombe yawls, a local class of racing boats, which evolved from the crabbing boats of the last century.

This area known as Dutch or Ditch End now has a landing stage and shelter erected by Portlemouth parishioners as a 1914-18 War Memorial.

In 1860 copper mining was carried out near here under the grand name of Portlemouth Consoles.

During a drought in 1858 Salcombe residents depended on a spring at Dutch End when their own springs failed.

Dutch End landing can be seen behind the steam yacht. In the foreground is the lifeboat *Alfred and Clara Heath* which came to Salcombe Station when it was reopened in 1930. She and subsequent lifeboats have been kept on a deep water mooring.

The first lifeboat *Rescue* came on station in 1869. She was followed by the *Lesty, William and Emma* and the *Sarah Ann Holden*. They were housed in the Lifeboat House at South Sands until the station was closed in 1925.

Fisherman's Cove, formally Stony Cove or Higher Passage Way, was the landing place for the flat-bottomed horse and cattle ferry. Doctor Vincent Twining and his coachman "Doctor" Jimmy Putt, with his pony and trap, used this ferry to cross the harbour to visit patients at Portlemouth.

In 1911 Salcombe firemen and their horse-drawn appliance went by this ferry to fight a fire at Small's House.

This is Ivy or Small's Cove with Ivy Cottage in the field above. On the shore is a little quay with a framework over which fishmen hung their nets to dry. Here was the original ferry landing and from the cove a pathway led to Portlemouth village. Today many feet of fine sand cover the rocky shore shown here.

When the pier was built it became the ferry landing place at Salcombe and the ferry boat crossed the harbour to a new landing stage at Ferryside, Portlemouth. The ferry shelter at Portlemouth was built by Commander S. W. Ryder when he introduced the motor ferry in 1911.

Portlemouth village, on the hill opposite Salcombe, provided a naval subsidy with Totnes, Brixham and Kingsbridge, when Dartmouth was unable to maintain a ship or its crew for Royal service during the Scottish War, 1310.

The village supplied twelve barges and one ballinger — a whaling boat — to transport the army to France at the start of the Hundred Years War, 1342. The Devonshire list of ships for the Crecy campaign of 1346 shows Portlemouth in fifth position. She supplied five ships and ninety-six men.

The church plate was pledged to raise the portion of money demanded from the village when a bulwark was built at the harbour mouth. Henry VIII, 1544.

Portlemouth was one of the villages from around the estuary which helped to fit out sixteen vessels to fight against the Armada in 1588.

Listed in William White's Directory of 1851 were two innkeepers, two blacksmiths and three shopkeepers.

The village extended down to Small's Cove until 1879. The pathway between the houses was a rough track of shallow steps cut from the rock.

When the Dowager Duchess died the Duke of Cleveland found the estate very neglected. His agents stated that if the village was to continue it had to be rebuilt.

To him this was needless expense as the tenants in the lower part of the village were fishermen and seamen who would not work on his land. Almost half the population was evicted and the houses demolished. Their plight was brought to public notice by Professor J. A. Froude, historian, who wrote to the national papers. 1880.

In 1881 the Duchess of Cleveland paid for the restoration of the parish church.

The rough outline of the demolished properties can still be seen from the present public path from Small's Cove to the village.

Edwin (Ned) Stone, an expert basket and crabpot maker, watches his grandchildren as they play inside a pot at Small's Cove. Busy fishermen's wives often put their babies inside crabpots using them as playpens, c. 1900.

The wall at Cable Cove displays a red board indicating the position of the submerged telegraph cable laid across the harbour.

Two famous "J" class racing yachts entered Salcombe harbour to shelter from a storm on 3rd September, 1934. Both were built in 1928 and were approximately eighty feet at the waterline and had one hundred and sixty feet masts.

Ager Point and Mill Bay seen from Rickham Golf Links during the 1920s. The links were closed at the onset of World War Two and were never reopened.

The stone wall some 12 feet high is now engulfed by sand. The concrete slipway seen on the beach today was made during World War Two by United States Naval Constructional Battalion (early 1944). Here damaged landing craft were repaired after the D-Day landings.

At the beginning of this century the sea reached the high wall at the top of Mill Bay. The accumulation of sand over the past eighty years has forced the stream to alter course from time to time. The source of the stream is in the valley below Rickham Farm but up to date we have found no records concerning a mill.

Regardless of the state of the tide, the stone barge *P.H.E.* discharged her cargo into a smaller barge. Then men loaded the stones into the cart which conveyed them up the beach for the construction of Mill Bay House, c. 1910.

Two elegantly dressed onlookers watch as local fishermen examine the catch in their tucking net which they have hauled at Biddle Head on the seaward side of Mill Bay, c. 1900.

Sunny Cove, as its name implies, is a sun trap and early this century a few summer visitors were on the beach. Occasionally the swell here makes the beaching of boats hazardous.

From 1893 the Great Western Railway brought goods to Kingsbridge but Salcombe still relied on trading vessels for the delivery of such items as coal, timber and building materials.

This photograph taken at the "Look Out" near the entrance to the Plantation Walk in Devon Road shows the broken water on the Bar and the rough water on the Hipple or Ripple Sands between Blackstone Rocks and Lambury Point.

A notice to mariners, issued 10th June, 1844, stated that the harbour was perfectly buoyed and beaconed. There was a black and white fairway buoy outside the Bar and a black buoy at Wolf Rock. Blackstone Rock had a beacon with two red balls on a crosstree. A beacon with one white ball was positioned on Poundstone, Old Harry and Muir's Rocks.

> Sunset and evening star,
>     And one clear call for me!
> And may there be no moaning of the Bar,
>     When I put out to sea.
>
> But such a tide as moving seems asleep,
>     Too full for sound and foam,
> When that which drew from out the boundless deep,
>     turns again home.
>
> Twilight and evening bell,
>     And after that the dark!
> And may there be no sadness of farewell
>     When I embark;
>
> For tho' from out our bourne of Time and Place,
>     The flood may bear me far,
> I hope to see my Pilot face to face,
>     When I have crost the Bar.
>
>         Alfred Lord Tennyson.

# Arthur L. Clamp – the man behind the books

Arthur Leslie Clamp was a man of boundless energy with a passion for helping others, particularly through his love of history. A printer by trade, he started his career in a printing company before moving his family from Exeter to Plymouth to teach at the Plymouth College of Art and Design, where he eventually became the Head of the Printing Department.

*Arthur with his five children.*

## A Devoted Family Man

Despite his love of teaching, Arthur prioritised his family, always making it home by 5:30pm for tea. He and his wife, Rosemary, raised five children: Susan, Angela, Elizabeth, David, and Steven. Arthur would often combine his love of family and history by taking his children on Sunday walks, encouraging them to appreciate historical monuments by taking photos or making crayon rubbings of gravestones for his books. The family home at 203 Elburton Road was a hub of activity, with a large garden, featuring a two-storey fort and a makeshift swimming pool.

## A Lifelong Learner and Adventurer

Arthur's thirst for knowledge extended beyond history to a deep curiosity about the world. He was passionate about exploring different cultures, traditions, and cuisines, often taking advantage of his long summer holidays as a teacher to travel to places like India, Russia, South America, the middle east and the USA, sometimes bringing one of his children along. This adventurous spirit even influenced his home life, as seen by the short-lived family tradition of steam-cooking vegetables after a trip to Iceland.

*History is a prominent feature of family days out*

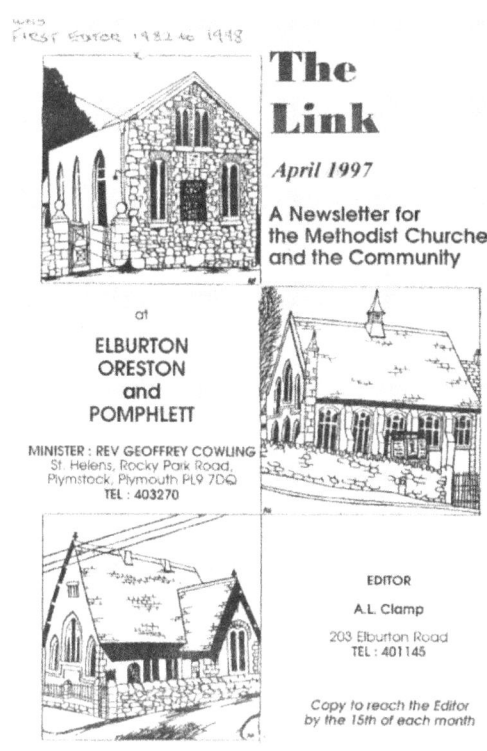

## Community and Philanthropic Spirit

His commitment to serving others was evident in his long-standing involvement with the Elburton Methodist Church. He was the Sunday School Superintendent for over 15 years and served as the editor of the wider church's monthly newsletter, "The Link," for a similar duration. After Rosemary's very sad passing, Arthur later remarried and, following a chance encounter with a professor from India, established a connection with a missionary school in Chennai. Together with his new wife, Christine, he co-founded a "Sponsor a Child's Education" program that continues to this day.

*Pictured left – The cover of 'The Link' complete
with hand drawn sketches of each church by Angela
Below right – Arthur Clamp promoting his latest book
Below left – Arthur at home with his first wife, Rosemary
Below centre – Arthur on holiday with his second wife, Christine*

## A Legacy of Learning and Positivity

Arthur's greatest passion was history, which he brought to life through tireless research, documentation, and the many books he authored. He was driven by a need to "never be stuck in a rut," constantly seeking new experiences, meeting new people, and expanding his knowledge. With a positive attitude and a great sense of humour, he was always ready to help others, leaving a lasting impact on his family and community. His children, Susan, Angela, Elizabeth, David, and Steven, remember him with love and gratitude.

David Clamp, 2025

# A Legacy of Local History

Below is the story of how Arthur L Clamp began writing books, in his own words, drafted shortly before he passed away in 2001. I have only made minor alterations to this text, correcting grammatical errors that he did not survive to correct himself. When I first discovered this text, I was shocked to see my name mentioned. It seems that, unbeknownst to me, I shared my first PC with him. I suspect he used it during the day when I was at school, although I do have one memory of sitting with him and showing him how it worked. It has been a pleasure to pick up where he left off and see his books republished and redistributed, and to know that I was part of the story, even back then. It was also fascinating to discover that his pricing structure matches the way I have tried to price the books, with a third going to local sellers and the rest covering printing costs with a little left over for my expenses.

I am his eldest grandson, and it is a privilege to curate his legacy, which we are calling 'The Clamp Collection'. The very last line of the text originally reads "The following pages list all the titles." Sadly, that page is missing and we have no record of all the books he published and knowing that some of those were researched by other authors makes the process of finding them even harder. I look forward to one day completing the collection and seeing them all available again. And maybe, one day, I'll even start writing my own to add to the series. For now, here is his story in his own words.

Steven Gibson, 2025

## Writing and Publishing Booklets on Local Topics and Areas

I started this interest in either 1968 or 1969 when living in Woodford. I had by these dates established the Department of Printing and I think I must have been looking for something different to do. The first titles were of A5 size proofed from type set at Clarke, Doble and Brendon, Ltd., Plymouth printers, and then made up into pages and printed at Sawtell and Neilson, Ltd., Totnes.

Then began a slow process of getting them out to shops, etc. which proved to be more time consuming and difficult than actually researching, writing and getting the books into print. However, I persisted and opened a business account with Barclays Bank on the Broadway. I was advised to give it a title so I called it "Westway Publications". There came along another problem, one of storage of paper and finished books which was solved when the family moved to Elburton in 1970.

I changed the printer to Penwell, Ltd., Callington, Cornwall, as he was then just setting up himself and his prices seemed very reasonable. I did not get any of the printers to make up the complete books. I hand folded the flat printed sheets, stitched the books on a small manual table stitcher and trimmed them in a small hand turned guillotine which I bought from someone in Penzance for £40. It was brought up in a van.

The trouble and time going to and fro to Callington was too much so I transferred the printing to PDS Printers, Prince Rock, Plymouth, and I have been with them ever since. Now they are at Plympton which is easy to reach and they fold the flat sheets which was turning out to be a long chore which only saved a small part of the printing costs.

All my first titles were written by myself. I took the photographs and developed them in the loft of the house, the type was set by now on a computer situated in the house at Elburton from which I had collected photographic lengths of text to cut up and law down as pages.

At some point I decided that I would do my own film processing of lith film so I bought a large second hand process camera from Kingsbridge and learnt through trial and error to make line negatives of the text and halftone negatives of the illustrations which proved more difficult than I anticipated. The main problem was trying to keep the developer in the large dish at the correct temperature as any change would affect the developing time. I replaced this old camera with a brand new one bought from Croydon, Surrey, costing £900. This has turned out to be a great asset cutting out an expensive part of the printer's costs and one crucial aspect of the work which I could control.

By the middle 1970s there were many outlets I had contacted in Plymouth, up to Dartmoor, Exeter, around to Torbay, Totnes, Dartmouth and the South Hams. The market for local books was much greater than I had first thought and through getting to know many local people undertaking research themselves had the chance to help and make up books for other people who had in most instances, got together a collection of photographs with some text in a rather muddled way. Through my experience in print I was able to shape up their work and get it into print and in every case I had to pay the printer and let the person have the royalties. In the majority of titles produced in this manner this was another way of producing titles and it did give some profit to my work. However, I must say that in a few cases I lost out by either the other person getting the numbers wrong, not returning any monies from stock I delivered or they thought that more of their books should have been sold.

The print run was usually 1,000 copies and from time to time I have had reprints of 250 copies. It took about ten years to clear the first print run so I always had large stocks in the garage, workshop, etc. The numbers sold during the early years was about 7,000 copies a year increasing to around 9,000 copies and for the whole of the enterprise about 500,000 have been sold. The booklets have become part of the local scene and many people collect them, shops regularly order copies and I go around certain areas month by month restocking or replacing titles as necessary.

During the past year or so I have started setting the text on a Packard Bell PC, something which I should have done some years back. I share it with Steven Gibson, my grandson. There appears to be no end to the market for local books, but I could not earn a regular income because of the long time it takes to sell stock.

However, now exceeding 100 titles made up mainly of A4 twenty-four page booklets, some folded guides, with selling prices set with a third going to the shop which is the trade custom, the original idea has been quite successful and could go on for ever.

Apart from monetary benefits, however spasmodically these might be, I have learnt a lot myself, met many interesting people and have become part of the local scene with requests to give talks and to advise people about getting into print.

Arthur L Clamp, 2001

## Death of local historical author

*'He was an incredible character who was just loved by everybody who knew him'*

This newspaper article, published by the Evening Herald on 17th August 2001, forms a good record of his life. Just as he encourages us to learn more about local history, we encourage you to learn a little about him. For that reason, we have included these pages at the back of all the most recently republished books, in honour of his memory and recognition of his contribution to the community.

www.ingramcontent.com/pod-product-compliance
Lightning Source LLC
Chambersburg PA
CBHW061405070526

44584CB00031B/4163